HOVE

A Pictorial History

Brunswick Square. Brunswick Town was the first of the major developments that were the key to the rapid expansion of Hove. Work on the Square began in 1825.

HOVE
A Pictorial History

Eddie Scott

Phillimore

1995

Published by
PHILLIMORE & CO. LTD.
Shopwyke Manor Barn, Chichester, West Sussex

ISBN 0 85033 981 2

Printed and bound in Great Britain by
BIDDLES LTD.
Guildford, Surrey

List of Illustrations

Frontispiece: Brunswick Square

Illustration Acknowledgements

The majority of the photographs and illustrations in this book appear by kind permission of Hove Central Library, East Sussex County Library. Because of this it seems sensible only to record the exceptions. The following appear with kind permission from: Ray Elliott, 152, 153, 154; Tony Howard, 25, 29, 30; Postcard Cabin, Queen's Road, Brighton (from whom copies can be obtained), 5, 29, 40, 42, 58, 67, 74, 80, 86, 97, 99, 105, 141, 149, 151; Borough of Hove Leisure Services Department, 180; the author, 23, 24, 33, 34, 47, 54-5, 56, 59, 60, 75-9, 82, 89, 98, 108, 109, 130, 136, 150, 159, 176, 177.

Acknowledgements

I would like to record my special thanks to the staff at Hove Central Library for their help and co-operation: the selection of illustrations would be immeasurably weakened without the support of the library. I would like to thank, too, Judy Middleton (who put me right on one or two things), Sian Watkins of Hove Borough Leisure Services Department (who kindly conducted me around the Old Shoreham Road Cemetery), Tony Howard (who enriched my understanding of Brunswick Town, where he has been in business for many years), and Tony Payne (who lent a knowledgeable ear to me). A book of this sort necessarily draws on the work of others. I am particularly indebted to Judy Middleton's *History of Hove*, the Portrait books of A.G. Elliott, and the article 'A Historical Geography of Urban Local Government in Sussex' by Donald F. Baxter (*Brighton Polytechnic Geographical Society Magazine*) which boosted my confidence that I had more or less sorted out the various Commissioners. I have drawn heavily from it for the introduction. Clifford Musgrave's *Life in Brighton* was helpful in understanding the early social connections between Hove and Brighton and D. Robert Elleray's recently published 'A Refuge from Reality: the Cinemas of Brighton and Hove' is an important source for cinema history and popular entertainment generally. I have also used Porter's *History of Hove*, the local newspapers (especially for the 1880s and '90s) and the local studies files in Hove Central Library.

Introduction

Hove is a town with an odd kind of history. Unlike towns such as Norwich or Chichester which have a long established geographical identity, the history of Hove is the story of the creation of a modern geographical identity from a small but ancient fishing village. In this sense its history is more like the growth of the modern industrial cities of Birmingham or Manchester. This is not, of course, to make too much of the comparison: Hove has never aspired to be an industrial town. The expansion of the village into a town over a short period is easily illustrated by the population statistics. In 1801, when Hove was just a cluster of houses around a single street, the population was 101 and in 10 years had grown to three times that size (312). By the end of the century the population was over 33,000 (33,284 in 1897).

An Expanding Village

Hove in 1995 is a collection of once-different places. The original parish of Hove, only a small part of which was occupied by the shore-line fishing village, has grown by the addition of Aldrington Parish (in 1893), the west part of Preston Rural Parish (in 1928), most of Blatchington County Parish (in 1928), all of Hangleton Parish (in 1928), a small part of Patcham County Parish (in 1928), three acres of Brighton Borough in exchange for a small part of Hove Borough in order to put the Dyke Road tram lines entirely within Brighton Borough, and in 1974 all of the Urban District of Portslade on Sea. If this was not complication enough, the original County of Hove parish has had within its boundaries three separate areas under Boards of Commissioners—Brunswick Square and Terrace Old Commissioners (from 1830), Brunswick Square and Terrace New Commissioners (taking in a larger area from 1851) and the West Hove Commissioners (taking in Cliftonville and Hove village from 1858). These three groups of Commissioners eventually combined to form the Hove Commissioners in 1874. The Hove Commissioners remained the principal civil authority until Urban District status was granted in 1894, with Municipal Borough status following in 1898.

The situation is still further complicated by the official church status of, first of all, Hove parish, but also of Aldrington and Hangleton parishes: as population decline and subsequent growth in these places, and later in Preston, caused parishes to be joined and subsequently separated.

From Commissioners to Borough

Up until the passing by Parliament of the Brunswick Square Act, in 1830, Hove parish had not been controlled by any real form of local government apart from the Overseers of the Poor Rate set up by Parliament for every parish. The duty of the Overseers was to collect a local tax and use it to relieve poverty in the parish. As the Overseers normally consisted of the wealthier parishioners, and therefore those eligible to pay for poor relief, they were taxed as lightly as possible. This resulted in poverty relief at the most basic level. In time it led to the idea of only offering help if the poor worked under supervision: so a poor family would find mother and children separated from father and each confined to single sex 'Work Houses'.

The setting up of Commissioners by act of Parliament created a more powerful instrument of local government. The act would set out the powers of the Commissioners, who were formally appointed by government, and answerable to Parliament for their decisions and conduct. In practice they governed by consent of the local landowners and business interests. Parliament granted powers to Commissioners for such things as town development, sewerage and water undertakings, policing and fire fighting. In the case of Hove the various Commissioners had overlapping powers and it was not until the combining of the separate Commissioner into the Hove Commissioners in 1874 that a recognisable form of local government came into being. Yet these Commissioners were still appointees, and the Board of Commissioners was rather like a modern quango. It was not until Hove became an urban district in 1894 that a more recognisable form of modern democratic local government was established.

Local Communities
This was the formal position. In practice people identified with different communities. Cliftonville, West Brighton, Aldrington and Hangleton are still seen by their residents as distinct communities, and within these somewhat loose descriptions there are separate community areas like 'Poets Corner' and 'Brunswick Town'. This identification with an organic community rather than an officially designated community is very common and can be found in many towns. In Newhaven (Sussex), for instance, there is still some locally recognised difference between those who live on the east or the west side of the river Ouse. To an outsider the differences may seem insignificant, but local people see it otherwise.

Within the new boundaries of the expanded Hove there were, or were to become, different geographical areas of economic activity which both reflected and helped to establish a local sense of place. There are several distinct shopping centres, each associated with different periods of town development, reflecting the neighbouring housing status, and to some extent catering for different consumer needs. Brunswick Town's purpose-built indoor market was designed to meet the needs of the grand houses of Brunswick Square and Terrace for everyday foodstuffs and household goods: grander purchases would come from London, or perhaps, Brighton. Blatchington Road developed as a shopping centre to meet all the requirements of a respectable middle- and working-class community. Post-war development at Hangleton has produced a shopping centre designed to meet the same type of need as the original Brunswick Town market. Portland Road was planned in order to meet the needs of the developing Stanford Estate. The shops of Western Road (including Palmeira House), as well as meeting mixed local needs, have always seen markets across the borough boundary in Brighton.

Grafted onto this domestic scene were those areas set aside in which the Victorians and Edwardians could pursue their summer social life: the various Lawns, Esplanades, Gardens and Parks. The social purpose of these facilities may have changed over the years, but they still form an obviously distinct area for sport, recreation and social life. It could hardly be different in a town that had grown up by the seaside.

Tucked away at the western end of Hove, and largely unnoticed by many, is the eastward end of Shoreham harbour. Although not now so busy, Aldrington Basin was once a thriving import depot for timber from the Baltic (much needed for the development of Hove and Brighton, as well as the expanding economy of the rest of the country) and coal, both for local domestic and commercial use.

A Patchwork Growth

The evolution of the variously distinct communities of Hove, is, of course, not without explanation. The success of the development of Brighton, fuelled by the popularity of Dr. Russell's sea-water cures, the subsequent adoption of the town for part of the fashionable season by the Prince Regent and his entourage, and the growing interest in sea bathing as a pleasure in itself, encouraged property developers to think of expanding Brighton westwards. The natural landscape of Brighton meant any large scale development would have to be to the west. With the completion of the laying out of Kemp Town estate to the east of Brighton there was no suitable land left in Brighton for similar developments. Immediately beyond Kemp Town the shingle beach gives way to the high chalk cliffs that run along the coast until the small gap at Rottingdean. Although development could have continued on the cliff top, as it has at Saltdean, Telscombe Cliffs and Peacehaven, these are essentially residential districts, not, despite much of the promotional material for these developments attempting to suggest otherwise, seaside places. To the north of Brighton's sea front the land soon becomes too hilly for grand schemes and building on hills is more expensive—but crucially, any development would be away from the sea front—the very impetus for more development.

In contrast the land to the west in Hove parish was relatively flat and virtually unused except for a brickworks, and it was unoccupied. Better still, the land was held by one owner, the Wick Estate.

The size of land holdings had been a problem for potential developers in Brighton, because most of the land surrounding the area of Brighton now known as Old Steine was held in small plots by many owners. This made the assembly of a large plot of land for a major development very difficult, and conversely made a large parcel of land held by a single, or just a few, owners attractive. Charles Busby and Amon Wilds could not have planned the vast undertaking of Brighton's Kemp Town without easy access to a large site, albeit some distance from the fashionable attractions of central Brighton and the Royal Pavilion.

The commercial urge to expand westward led Busby and Wilds to conceive the idea of building a complimentary west wing to Brighton's east wing, Kemp Town. They were commissioned to build a similar estate to Kemp Town in the parish of Hove at the western end of the Western Road. The building of Brunswick Square and Brunswick Terrace started in 1824 and, although conceived as the western extension and complementary to east Brighton, was to become the first stage in what was to become the fast growing town of Hove.

More Patches

The remainder of the Wick Estate was purchased in 1830 by Baron Goldsmid. Work on this new development, which we know as Adelaide Crescent and Square, began in 1830. The architect for this next major patchwork piece in the development of Hove was Decimus Burton, who had previously built Wick Hall for the Baron. Burton was then fashionable as an architect, only recently having been responsible for planning Hyde Park in London. With the near completion of the Wick Estate's seaside land by the end of the 1850s, the development of Brunswick and Adelaide was nearly completed.

The next patch in the quilt to be developed was the land adjacent to the east side of Hove village. Unlike the land that the Brunswick Estate was built on, this was good agricultural land that had more recently be turned into market gardening and nursery use to meet the needs of the Brunswick and Palmeira developments. This area, to become known as Cliftonville, was developed by a small consortium of Brighton businessmen as a building speculation. Although the estate was successfully completed in the 1850s, and is now largely a conservation area, the original partners failed to make their hoped for fortune from the project.

With the completion of Brunswick and Adelaide estates in the east and the new estate of Cliftonville in the west of the parish, the sea-front terraces had a wide gap in the middle. This was developed, as West Brighton Estate, in the period between 1875 and about 1910. It includes the four great avenues that flank Grand Avenue and with its completion the continuous façade of grand structures ran uninterrupted from the Brighton boundary almost to humble Hove Street.

The Stanford Estate, the largest in area of all the Hove land holdings, had the disadvantage of lying a little inland. However, once the shore developments were well underway, there grew a demand to develop the land behind the seaside estates, partly to provide accommodation for the many workers the grand avenues, terraces and squares required to support them. The Stanford Estate, lying mostly north of Church Road, included the area between Sackville Road and the Drive. This area of Hove was developed in the 1870s and 1890s.

These estates, Brunswick, Adelaide (Goldsmid), Cliftonville, West Brighton and Stanfield were the major patches in the quiltwork pattern that became Hove up until 1911. Smaller patches were added at the fringes of the old parish of Hove until the outbreak of the First World War. The next major additions to the pattern were the full development of Aldrington and Hangleton parishes and the incorporation in 1974 of Portslade.

The Consequences

The development of Hove in these large patches enabled the town to be built to an evolving rational plan. This is not to say that there was ever any master blueprint, but rather that, although each of the major developments sought to be self sufficient to some degree (in the case of Brunswick, totally self sufficient), each new development could hardly ignore what had gone before: and so a more coherent town was developed than in neighbouring Brighton. Of the three major modern towns of East Sussex—Hove, Brighton and Eastbourne—the pattern of land tenure has been a highly significant factor in the eventual pattern of urban development. In Eastbourne, where there were only three large landowners, and those dominated by the Cavendish estates, the land-owners collaborated in planning a town fit for the genteel. Their plan has effectively been carried out. Hove, without any one dominating landowner (and originally conceived by Brighton developers as an adjunct to Brighton), was nevertheless developed with a certain degree of consistency. The fragmentary land holdings in the older part of Brighton created a different and less ordered plan of development. The later Hove estates were created on formal grid patterns, perhaps revealing an acquaintance with trans-Atlantic ideas of town planning: although Roman town patterns in England could equally have provided a model. It may be that the availability of large tracts of fairly flat lands could be best economically exploited by a grid system.

Growing Pains

The rapid growth of Hove was inevitably to cause problems, especially as this growth was to lead to the most densely populated local government area of East Sussex. Even the very sparsely populated old village of Hove had problems with its water supply. There were wells at the northern and southern ends of Hove Street, which were normally sufficient for the domestic and agricultural needs of the village, but following a big storm the southern well was spoiled and new supplies had to be found. If the small village of Hove had problems, it takes no imagination to realise the scale of the problem of water supply to a large town.

Water supply is obviously not the only requirement. The disposal of water in the form of sewerage is no less important. This was a special problem for a town developed on land only a few feet above sea level, as the gradient for large parts of the seaside area of Hove provided only minimal natural drainage. What natural drainage there was led to the beach. This was sufficient for a small community, but became unacceptable as the town grew: not least because it was the pleasures of the beach and sea front that had been the cause of that growth. The problem of satisfactory sewerage disposal was to lead to a lengthy legal dispute. Hove and Brighton had a joint agreement on its disposal and had shared the cost of building a sewer along the sea front to intercept the road drains and sewers flowing down to the beach. This intercepting sewer discharged at Portobello, well to the west of Brighton. When Aldrington was absorbed into Hove and subsequently extensively developed, Hove wanted to add Aldrington's sewerage to the intercepting sewer. Engineers engaged by Brighton argued that the existing arrangements could not cope and that Aldrington's sewerage should be discharged at Shoreham. Hove stuck by the agreement that Hove sewerage should go via the intercepting sewer. Of course the underlying problem was that if the sewerage system had to be upgraded, then the costs would largely fall on Brighton. Eventually the matter was pursued through the courts to the ultimate appeal—to the House of Lords— who found in Hove's favour.

The need for what today we call infrastructure became more pressing each year. At first the water needs were met by sinking wells. By 1836 the Brighton, Hove and Preston Water Works was formed to meet the growing demand, but this provided insufficient supplies and in 1862 the West Brighton Water Company bought land at Goldstone bottom on the advice of the engineer, Thomas Hawksley. Hawksley had been the engineer responsible for providing water supplies to Nottingham, Liverpool and Sheffield. In 1876 he was President of the Institute of Mechanical Engineers. The existing pumping station (now the Engineerium) was built in 1866 to house the steam-driven beam engines which pumped water from a well over fifty metres deep.

Other amenities followed. School boards were set up to provide education for every child, the police force was expanded, fire services were developed (although horse-drawn appliances were still being used up to the outbreak of the First World War) and public transport systems were set up. The issue of public transport, the type of vehicles to use—horse-drawn buses, motor buses, horse trams, motor trams or electric trolley buses—drew fierce debates in the local press and in the council chambers. The arguments over whether Hove Corporation should provide transport services or whether private enterprise echo down the years to today.

Conflict with Brighton

The difference that arose between Hove and Brighton over the intercepting sewer was by no means the only cause of friction. Not unnaturally, attempts were made to incorporate West Brighton, in Hove parish, into Brighton. When Hove applied for a charter in 1896 to become a borough, Brighton gave evidence to the Commission set up by the Privy Council to the effect that Hove should become part of Brighton. This was rejected by the Commission as were earlier suggestions for incorporating the part of Hove parish that was called West Brighton. As this introduction is concluded the same argument for combining the two towns is under discussion. Hove has created a distinct style, different from that of Brighton, and its people are understandably anxious to retain that sense of difference.

Hove Village

1 This view of Hove Street, taken in September 1914, looking south, shows the partial development of the street at that time. Hove Manor is the large building on the left-hand side of the Street. The building opposite (in the centre of the picture) is Hove Cottage. On the right of the picture is part of the frontage of the recently built *Connaught Hotel*. Building work is in progress next to the *Connaught*.

2 This view, taken further down towards the sea, shows the twist in the original course of Hove Street. Hove Manor was built in 1785 by John Vallance who owned farmlands nearby. Further down the Street, on the right, was Hove Lodge which at the time of this picture was used as a school. The two youngsters in the foreground are delivery boys—probably delivering bread and meat.

3 This view of the Manor, taken from the gardens of Hove Cottage, gives a better idea of the style of the building, which, when the village was virtually confined to Hove Street, would have been very impressive. At the time this picture was taken (September 1914) Hove Cottage is in a poor state of repair. The top of the gasometer can be glimpsed above the roofs.

4 The Manor, originally known as Hove House, changed name when John Olliver Vallance bought the rights to the Lordship of the Manor. The attractive exterior was matched by the interior which boasted panelled rooms and a Chippendale staircase. Part of the house is thought to be built from stone and flints from an old ecclesiastical building that stood a little to the north.

5 The old *Ship Inn*, built in 1702, stood almost at the bottom of Hove Street, just above the coastguard station. This picture, looking northwards, clearly shows the curve to the right before this part of the street was straightened. In the 18th and early 19th centuries the *Ship* was a centre for bull-baiting. The present building is on the site of the older inn.

6 The *Ship Inn* is the oldest pub site in Hove, although this building is not the present pub, which was built in the early 1910s. The West Street Brewery, whose ales the *Ship* sold, was a family business of the Vallance family of Hove Manor—not a stone's-throw away. The first *Ship Inn* was built in 1702 to serve the local fishermen and later smugglers who landed their contraband cargoes of French spirits on the beach at night. The pub was rebuilt in 1808. The building, photographed *c.*1912, was demolished in 1915 in order to straighten the road

7 This picture of a cow and its calf was taken *c.*1912. The picture was taken from the Hove Street end of what is now Vallance Road and reminds us of the essentially rural nature of early Hove. The houses in the background are in the newly-developed Aymer Road.

8 The Vallance family moved to Hove from Patcham in the 1780s and a John Vallance built the Manor, probably around 1785. The Vallance family, in association with the Killicks and later the Catts, were Brighton brewers. Their West Street Brewery was one of the oldest in Brighton though not old fashioned. The portrait is of John Olliver Vallance (1847-1893) and was taken *c*.1870.

9 This domestic scene of the Vallance family children playing in the field behind the Manor was taken in early spring 1910. The fine cupola (or small bell tower) finely balances the gable-end chimneys of this attractive house.

10 The Vallance family were keen huntsmen and John Brooker Vallance started the Brighton Harriers who chased hares for sport. This picture, taken in 1867, shows Mr. and Mrs. Olliver and their daughter, Mrs. Sarah Duke Vallance, outside the back of Hove Manor with the hunt.

11 The boatyard, photographed in 1908, was a necessary part of any fishing community for building, maintenance and supplies. Thwaites stood near the beach, south of the Shoreham Road (soon to be re-named Kingsway in honour of visits to Hove by King Edward VII) near the coastguard station.

12 This row of cottages, known informally as Beach Cottages, stood south of the Shoreham Road, below the coastguard station. The coastguard station opened in 1831 as part of a concerted effort by Parliament to reduce smuggling. This view, photographed *c.*1910, shows the west side of the cottages with a surveyor's assistant standing at the back of the cottages.

13 This view of the Cottages, taken from the east, shows them shortly before their demolition. In fact the surveyor's assistant from the previous picture is helping to survey the area prior to widening the Shoreham Road.

14 The need to demolish the Beach Cottages in order to widen the Shoreham Road is obvious from this photograph. The north side of the road has been paved and provided with gas lights, the south side remains unpaved. The tall pipe just beyond the first gas lamp is a vent to the sewer that ran, and still runs, beneath Hove Street.

15 This tithe barn was used to store the farm produce required by the church from each farm in the parish. The tax was set at one tenth. The barn was very near the present library, just south of Connaught Street. This building, together with the Prebend House which stood nearby and St Andrew's Church, were the religious quarter of old Hove. The barn was eventually pulled down when Church Road was widened in 1895. The photograph was taken shortly before.

16 Hove church, Hove Old Church and St Andrew's are names given to the same church, although it has gone through several transformations. It was recorded as being in ruins in the late 16th century. This print, which must precede the restoration of 1836, shows the ruins of the tower and the re-built smaller church.

17 This picture, drawn earlier than the previous one, shows St Andrew's Church without the small tower and with more of the old tower. The stones from this tower made useful building material and were recycled into other buildings, including those of Goodwood Park estate.

18 This engraving, looking towards the north-east, shows the restored parish church of old Hove. In the distance can just be seen the windmills of modern-day Preston and Hollingbury.

19 This view of St Andrew's, from the north, shows part of the extensive graveyard. The south side, too, was once comparatively large, but was reduced by the need to widen Church Road. In the graveyard is buried one of the most famous names in the world—Sir George Everest, Surveyor-General of India—after whom the world's highest mountain is named.

20 This distant view from an old watercolour shows St Andrew's after restoration, and a few adjacent buildings in Hove Street. In the foreground is Long Barn Farm, part of the Wick Estate, at what became the junction of Wilbury and Eaton Roads. This picture was painted in the late 1830s.

Brunswick Town and West Brighton

21 This painting of a general view of Hove of *c*.1840 is seen from further towards Brighton than the previous picture. The restored St Andrew's is in the distance by Hove Street and on the left the nearly completed Brunswick Square serves to show how far the first modern development was from the old village of Hove.

22 The elegant Brunswick Square was finished in 1828. It stands on lands that were part of the Wick Estate which were formerly used for growing flax and making bricks. The principal architect was Charles Augustus Busby, who with Amon Wilds, a Lewes man, was responsible for the development of Kemp Town.

23 Adelaide Crescent and Brunswick Square and Terrace formed the public face of Brunswick Town. Behind these grand façades more humble streets provided for the needs of the rich. Many famous people have lived in these prestigious houses: perhaps few more colourful than Barney Barnato—the Gold King— associate of Cecil Rhodes and founder of the Kimberley Diamond Mining Company.

24 Work on Brunswick Terrace begun in 1824 and was not finished until 1827. The terrace and square provide the most distinguished architecture of 19th-century Hove. Surprisingly, despite the grandeur of the two terraces, Hove Council once considered their demolition to make way for high-rise flats, and in the face of opposition proposed instead to turn the gardens into a car park!

25 The fame of West Brighton's magnificent squares and terraces spread throughout Europe and attracted many foreign visitors, both for the curative values of sea water and the fashionable scene. This German engraving, produced before the West Pier was built in 1866, shows Brunswick Terrace with the old Chain Pier in Brighton just visible.

26 This was Hove's first Town Hall, photographed in September 1957, although it started out as the headquarters of the Brunswick Commissioners. It was built in 1855 and still stands in Brunswick Street West. When the Commissioners became part of Hove this building became the Town Hall. A police station and fire service were also part of the same location.

27 Du Pont's West Brighton Riding Academy was in Lower Market Street and Waterloo Street. It advertised as being 'By Appointment to the International Polo Club' and was headquarters of the Yeomanry. It hired and sold horses and carriages and provided stabling and rooms for coachmen. The building was opened on 30 October 1828 as a market for Brunswick Town.

28 Waterloo Street was part of Brunswick Town, but the land on which the Italianate St Andrew's Church (in the centre of the picture) was built was owned by the Rev. Edward Everard, not the main developers. The architect was Sir Charles Barry, builder of the gothic St Peter's in Brighton and the even more gothic Houses of Parliament.

29 Opposite St Andrew's Church in Waterloo Street stands the public house now called the *Iron Duke* after the victor of the Battle of Waterloo. This is a recent name. It originally opened, before 1828, as the *Kerrison Arms* (Sir Edward Kerrison, a Hove resident, had fought with Wellington in the Peninsular War). In 1910 it was renamed the *Hove Lawns Hotel* and advertised 'Billiards and Pyramids'—a form of billiards played with 15 coloured balls.

30 This picture shows the *Lawns Hotel* in Waterloo Street shortly after a fire. A policeman stands by the entrance to discourage looters and a fireman poses for the photographer on the corner of Brunswick Street East. The photographer has used the earlier name *Kerrison Arms* to identify the picture.

31 The side streets, or mews, that were created to serve the grand terraces and squares of Brunswick Town are well illustrated by this 1960s picture of Brunswick Street West, the street where the Brunswick Commissioners had their headquarters. The name Brunswick was taken from the Prince Regent's wife, Caroline of Brunswick.

32 From its beginning Brunswick Town had been developed with a view to attracting short-term residents, unlike neighbouring Kemp Town in Brighton, where the developers had permanent residences in mind. The Dudley Mansion in Lansdowne Place met this requirement. This advertisement, from a directory, shows that early Brunswick Town considered itself part of Brighton.

DUDLEY MANSION.

52, 55 & 57, LANSDOWNE PLACE

WEST BRIGHTON.

PRIVATE

Boarding Establishment

PRIVATE APARTMENTS WITH OR WITHOUT BOARD.

Near the Sea & Esplanade,

TARIFF SENT ON APPLICATION.

COMFORTABLE READING ROOM AND ELEGANT DRAWING ROOM.

A. F. LAMETTE, Proprietor.

33 The *Dudley Hotel*, formerly Dudley Mansion, in Lansdowne Place was one of Brunswick's premier hotels. While not one of the town's most fashionable addresses, Lansdowne Place was nevertheless 'respectable'—in fact the novelist Charles Dickens is reputed to have stayed there with his friend, the cartoonist, John Leech.

34 Palmeira Square acts as link between the old Hove and Brunswick Town. It was built between 1855 and 1870 but had earlier been the site of an ambitious project to build a huge glass-domed conservatory, called the Anthaeum (*sic*). Amon Wilds, of Kemp Town fame, was the architect, but he resigned when the developers altered his design. The structure collapsed the day before the official opening.

35 St John the Baptist Church stands at the western end of Palmeira Square and is the only prominent church with a significant spire. At the eastern end the square is dominated by Palmeira House, visible just off-centre.

Palmeira House, Western Road, Brighton.
STORES FOUNDED 1873.

36 Brighton and Hove Co-operative Supply Association's large store on the corner of Palmeira Square and Western Road has been called the Harrod's of Hove. Indeed they did boast to supply anything and even included a reading room and the facility to buy and sell shares on the London exchange. In 1891 'Fine Cognac' was available at £1 a gallon.

37 Holland Road, like Lansdowne Place, was a street that catered for the visitor to what, in the 1870s, was still known as West Brighton. Holland House sets out its charms in this advert. Holland Road can lay claims to be the site of the first cricket ground in Hove—Jem Nye's cricket field is marked on a map of 1844 opposite the *Wick Inn.* Nye was landlord of the *Wick.*

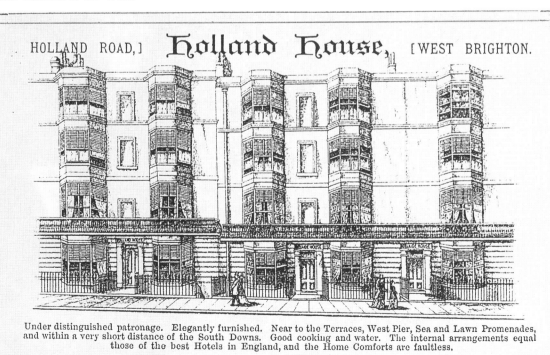

HOLLAND ROAD,] **Holland House,** [WEST BRIGHTON.

[67]

Under distinguished patronage. Elegantly furnished. Near to the Terraces, West Pier, Sea and Lawn Promenades, and within a very short distance of the South Downs. Good cooking and water. The internal arrangements equal those of the best Hotels in England, and the Home Comforts are faultless.

38 This developer's plans for Furze Hill gives a clear idea of how living at Hove was projected in the late 1870s to would-be residents. In fact this was supposed to be a 'village' offering the perceived benefits of village life together with close proximity to the urban sophistication of Brighton. The rest of Hove has almost disappeared and Shoreham sits in a wide bay!

Cliftonville and West Brighton

39   This view, looking northwards, shows the restored St Andrew's Church with St Andrew's School to the east and a brewery to the west. In the field in front of the church archery targets are set up. This field was where the Hove Toxophilite Society (founded in 1863) met for practice and competitions.

40   This early summer morning picture shows two of the streets of Cliftonville: Osborne and Medina Villas. In the background the old Town Hall clock tower can be seen, and nearby, to the left, is the Catholic Church of the Sacred Heart.

41   Victoria Terrace, together with the adjacent Courtney Terrace, were exceptional in that they faced away from the sea. They formed the only substantial buildings between the Shoreham Road and the seafront. Unlike the other main terraces, their purpose was not just residential. Victoria Terrace, shown here, was developed in the 1890s and contains workshops, pubs, shops and an early garage to serve the new motor trade.

42 The *Sussex Hotel* stands at the junction of Osborne Villas and what was the Shoreham Road when this picture was taken in the winter snow. Behind the hotel, on Osborne Villas were the hotel stables and a vetinerary surgery for horses and pets which was operated by W.K. Stuart. It is easy to forget how important horses were to people at this time.

43 The coastal road which was once known as the Shoreham Road was renamed Kingsway in 1910 in honour of the visits to Hove of King Edward VII, particularly as he frequently stayed in the part of the town shown in this picture of West Brighton taken from Courtney Terrace in 1910. On the seaward side (not shown) are the King's Lawns and the promenade or esplanade. On the north side are the southern entrances to Fourth, Third and Grand Avenues. A 'Corporation of Hove' general purpose wagon is turning off Kingsway, while a motor bus chugs towards Shoreham.

44 This picture of Kingsway was taken a little after the previous one, which, by looking in the opposite direction, complements it. The inland side of the picture shows the edge of Adelaide Crescent and the entrances to St John's Road, First, Second and Grand Avenues. In the distance beyond King's Lawns is Medina Terrace. This area became famous as the favoured area of the wealthy Sassoon family. King Edward VII stayed several times here at King's Gardens with his friend Arthur Sassoon. The family wealth was based on the fortune amassed by Sir Albert Sassoon as a merchant in Bombay. Their wealth, their association with the king through his friendship with Arthur and Rueben Sassoon, and their extensive cultural circle ensured the family a prominent place in court life. The king found Rueben's knowledge of horse racing useful too.

45 This scene from the 1890s of the south end of Grand Avenue, the grandest of the West Brighton avenues, shows the statue erected to commemorate Queen Victoria's 60 years on the throne. It was unveiled in 1901 shortly after she had died. The large building behind the Queen's statue was commandeered by the Royal Navy in the Second World War and became H.M.S. *Lizard* until 1948.

46 All Saints' Church in Eaton Road was completed in 1909. The architect J.L. Pearson was also responsible for the design of Truro Cathedral. The style is a mixture of traditional and Victorian ideas of gothic. In many ways a splendid building, it still lacks the tower of the original design.

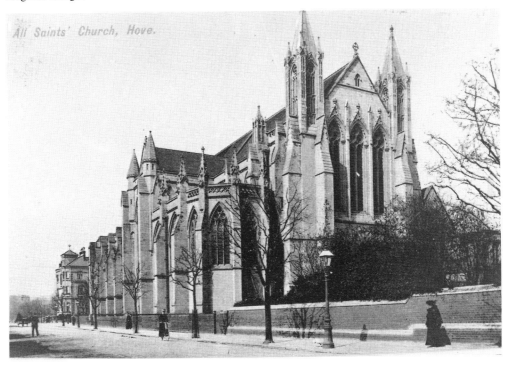

47 Grand Avenue was built to be impressive, although some of the houses were considered to be designed in too ornate a style. Unlike the surrounding First, Second, Third and Fourth Avenues, Grand Avenue has been subjected to extensive redevelopment in the form of dull blocks of flats, and little remains of the original avenue.

48 The proprietor of the *Rosstrevor Hotel*, Alfred Lucas, was typical of many occupiers of premises in the West Brighton area in the 1880s in offering hotel, but particularly boarding accommodation. Those who could afford to would spend their summer weeks at Hove for their health, the social life and what today we would call net-working. Presumably sea water for the baths was fetched as required.

Aldrington

49 Aldrington's early history is something of a mystery. It has been suggested that it was once an important Roman strategic settlement, Portus Adurni, but the matter is obscure because coastal erosion and drifting shingle have caused the river Adur to change its course over the years. It is known that the population of the parish fluctuated dramatically, dwindling at one stage to one. The ruin of the church and the loss of population were due to loss of farmland to sea erosion.

50 This photograph, looking towards the east of the ruins of the old church, was taken in about 1860. If you look carefully you can see a seated woman amongst the ruins. At this time the population of Aldrington was less than ten, but a few years earlier it had consisted of only one, Michael Maynard, the one-legged turnpike gate (or toll gate) keeper. In his *History of Sussex*, 1870, Lower remarks that the population could be described as three-quarters!

51 This early print of a carriage heading westward along the Shoreham Road gives Aldrington a very Regency look. The house in the foreground would have stood close to the *Mariners Arms* by the Aldrington parish boundary. St Andrew's Church in the background is in its partially restored state which shows that the print pre-dates the 1836 restoration. In fact the print dates from *c.*1820.

52 This panoramic view of Aldrington, taken around the turn of the century and photographed from near Aldrington recreation ground, shows New Church Road lined with young trees and provided with gas lighting—all ready for development. The church is the then recently built St Phillip's. The houses behind the church are in Glebe Villas. Kenya and Derek Avenues have been laid out and await their houses.

53 The Aldrington parish church, St Philip's, was built in 1895 and further expanded in 1910. The architect was J. Oldrid Scott, son of Sir George Gilbert Scott, architect of the Albert Memorial in London. The style is typical of Oldrid Scott's work, using a wide variety of building materials to produce a multi-coloured building and using these to produce ornamentation rather than adding ornamentation to the structure. The basic materials are brick, Bath stone, grey limestone and flint.

54 The elegant terraces of West Brighton and Cliftonville eventually extended along the Shoreham Road into the newly-absorbed parish of Aldrington. These terraces were built as private homes, but the four houses, built in 1904, in the smaller of the two terraces shown in this picture became the *Sackville Hotel*.

55 The manner of Hove's development, with large swathes like Brunswick, Cliftonville and Aldrington being developed at different times, has resulted in a fragmented shopping scene, as shops were provided for each new development in turn. Portland Road was developed as the shopping and entertainment area for the Vallance Estate in Aldrington. The large building on the right of the picture is the Police Seaside Home, which once had a clear view to the sea. In the late 1890s future traffic problems were remote.

POLICE SEASIDE H
HOVE BRIGH

56   The Police Seaside Home was built for convalescing policemen from all over the country. The Home is a large red-brick structure on the northside of Portland Road at the Sackville Road end. The architect was J.C. Gibbon. The Home was opened in 1893 by the Countess of Chichester. During the First World War it was used for wounded soldiers. The Home has since moved to Kingsway and this building has found other uses.

57 There once stood in what came to be called Goldstone Valley a group of large stones, the largest of which was called the Goldstone. It, and its smaller partners, have been identified as a pagan Druid site. By 1833 its fame was sufficient for Farmer Rigden to become so annoyed by sightseers from Brighton to have the stones buried to protect his crops. Later antiquarian interest prompted Hove councillor, Mr. Hollamby, to have it dug up and now it is placed in Hove Park. The figure in the foreground with a stick is Farmer Cornford. The Brighton and Hove Albion Football Club ground takes its name from these ancient stones. This picture, taken on 29 September 1900, shows workmen digging up the Goldstone. In 1906 the stones were placed in the newly-opened Hove Park.

West Blatchington and Hangleton

58 When sheep were regularly moved over the Downs they used tracks called droveways and the names of many local roads echo this past use. The Droveway was one such route. This photograph, taken *c*.1903, from near the top of The Droveway (with Dyke Road just a little behind the photographer) shows the road running down to Brighton Corporation's Goldstone Water Works (now the Engineerium). The buildings are Preston Farm, now a dairy depot. Elrington Road now joins where the little clump of trees stands.

59 St Peter's Church, West Blatchington, like nearby St Helen's at Hangleton, was once in ruins and was used to keep chickens whilst the tiny congregation held their services elsewhere. The building, which still retains some Norman elements, was restored in 1876 and, when the population of the parish greatly expanded in the late 19th and early 20th centuries, this little church was extended.

60 The sight of draught horses would once have been very familiar around the sunken lanes of West Blatchington and Hangleton. They would usually work in pairs, the same team always working together. This pair is just coming up from Toad's Hole on their way to West Blatchington village. The road to Red Hill, Westdene and Dyke Road Avenue has now been superseded by King George VI Avenue, built in the late 1930s. The horses stand near the present junction between Nevill Road and Goldstone Crescent.

61 This old photograph shows the Piggeries in the mid-1860s. They were at the top of Sackville Road, just off the old Shoreham Road. There was, a little earlier in 1844, another piggery in what was to become Adelaide Crescent. Piggeries were pig farms where the pigs were kept in pens rather than free-range. They needed less land and could be fed for the requirements of the table more easily. An old quarry has been put to good use to make caves for the pigs.

62 This picture of Hangleton Manor and village, taken in 1918, is looking west from West Blatchington. Beyond the Manor, on the horizon, can be seen the buildings of the Hangleton Isolation Hospital. It was common practice in late Victorian times to build such hospitals away from population centres, as it was thought that this would help to prevent infectious diseases from spreading. The spread of disease from the poor to the affluent was a very real fear for the town's wealthier residents.

63 St Helen's Church, Hangleton, stands a little way off from the settlement around the Manor, but once a thriving village clustered by the church. Fire and the Black Death have been suggested as the causes for the decline in population, but the young men may just have left to find work elsewhere. Whatever the reason, the church fell into disrepair as this print of 1851 by R.H. Nibbs shows. Parts of the church date from Saxon times, although most of the building is Norman.

64 The choice of St Helen as the patron saint for Hangleton church is unusual. St Helen is thought to have been a British woman who married a Roman and became the mother of Constantine the Great. Certainly there are many Roman connections on the area, including the site of a Roman villa less than half a mile away. When the population of the parish declined the church decayed and the tower was open to the sky. It was restored in 1876 when a small spire was added to weatherproof the tower.

65 Hangleton Manor, for many years the oldest inhabited building in Hove, dates back to the mid-16th century, although the manor itself is much earlier and is mentioned in Domesday Book (1086). Then it was a substantial holding, having enough land for eight ploughs. William the Conqueror granted the manor to William de Wateville. Over the centuries the manor has been lived in by many famous families—the Bellinghams, the Sackvilles and the Poynings amongst them. The Poynings family (originally De Poynings) were descended from a follower of William the Conqueror. A Michael De Poynings fought at Crecy in 1346. Another, Thomas Poynings, distinguished himself at the Battle of Boulogne, 1545. The Bellinghams (originally De Bellingham) were descended from Alan, who came from Normandy with William the Conqueror. Sir Edward Bellingham was another who fought at the Battle of Boulogne. The Sackville family held the Manor for over three hundred years. Sir Richard Sackville, a cousin of Anne Boleyn, was a Member of Parliament for Sussex.

66 The Manor was the centre of a large farm and, over the years, outbuildings and cottages were added. Cereal crops and sheep farming were the principal activity of the manor and other local farms, and this was profitable enough for Richard Bellingham to build the present manor, using stone from Lewes Priory, recently (1537) demolished following the Dissolution of the Monasteries. Flint buildings are greatly strengthened if their corners, doorways and windows can be fashioned from brick or stone. The low building on the right is a modern addition.

67 The Manor farm buildings lay in a small valley, surrounded by trees and in some considerable isolation until the 1940s. This picture clearly shows how stone from Lewes Priory was used to frame the main entrance. This tranquil scene belies the effort that has been going on inside. Hand-washing was heavy work and best attended to after a day's rest; this meant that Mondays were inevitably the day for washing.

68 The post-war development of Hangleton changed a sleepy depopulated village into a bustling modern suburb. This 1950s view of West Way shows the hillside in the distance as bare farmland: now the houses of Mile Oak cover it. The bus, then as now a number five, has stopped by Dale View. The wasteland in the foreground is the site of the track of the closed Dyke Railway.

The Seafront

69 This print of Hove beach, by Nibbs, shows how simple the sea defences were in 1840. There is a rudimentary wall in front of the buildings, but to the east side there is no wall and shrubs grow at high-water mark. In the distance (to the right of the picture) the recently restored St Andrew's Church can be seen across the field that one day would become part of Cliftonville.

70 A great storm on 1 September 1883 destroyed the temporary sea defences and prompted the authorities to build a secure wall. This wall, and more particularly the land it created, has played a major part in establishing Hove as a desirable residential resort. This photograph, taken in 1885, shows the building of the new sea wall. The steam engine on the left is pile-driving the new piles. The remains of the previous sea wall can be seen in the line of piles running just in front of the engine.

71 This picture clearly shows the problems that the relentless attrition of the sea causes to low coastlines like Hove's. The sea, even on a low tide, is very close to the promenade and threatens the sea defences; so much so that shingle is being heaped against the sea wall in order to protect the wall itself. This can only be a temporary measure as one storm will wash all this away.

THE BEACH & KINGS ESPANADE, HOVE.

72 (*above left*) By May 1885 the new sea wall was nearing completion. The flint-faced blocks of the wall have been laid and work is concentrated on laying the asphalt finish to the new promenade. This major engineering work guaranteed the threatened lawns of Brunswick and West Brighton and added a wide promenade for the society figures of Hove to meet and stroll.

73 (*above*) This postcard shows the new sea wall with ornamental iron railing added to the granite coping of the wall. Four flights of steps were included in the works to provide access to the beach. The gain in land can clearly be seen and the distancing of the breaking surf from the terraces of Kingsway was an additional advantage.

74 (*left*) The new sea wall secured the safety of the battery and coastguard station from the ravages of the sea. The guns of the battery have their barrels protruding from the slightly-built wooden building behind the signalling rostrum. By the flag-mast sits a howitzer. At the time (*c.*1920) the battery had no offensive or defensive rôle. The battery developed from the days when the coastguard was reorganised in 1856 and when men were recruited exclusively from the Royal Navy and the service formed a Naval Reserve. The coastguard service was run by the Admiralty and ex-Naval guns were installed to keep up the training of the Reserve

75 The popularity of sea bathing, which we take so naturally for granted, owes its origin to a treatise published in Latin by a then little-known doctor from Lewes. Dr. Richard Russell's book published by Oxford University in 1750, and quickly republished in English in an anonymous and unauthorised edition in 1752, titled *Dissertation on the Use of Sea Waters in the Diseases of the Glands*, was to lead to the phenomenal growth of Brighton and other seaside towns, not least neighbouring Hove. Quite why Russell's book was to spark this enthusiasm for sea bathing is difficult to understand because drinking and bathing in fresh sea water was only one part of his recommended cures: sea water was to be drunk with other concoctions such as crab's eyes and snails and no cure would be complete without the usual blood letting. Perhaps it was the prospect of a stay by the sea that made his course of treatment more palatable than that of his contemporaries.

76 Bathing machines were a Regency device for conveying the sick and infirm across the beach to the sea edge, but they also served to meet the proprieties of Victorian and Edwardian sensibilities towards less than fully-clothed bodies. One entered the machine at the top of the beach, changed into swimwear, and was then pushed to the water's edge where a few short steps down the ladder would quickly conceal the body in the sea. Mixed bathing from machines, which eventually came, was viewed with suspicion, as was the later arrival of nude bathing.

77 The new esplanade created by the new sea wall is well illustrated in this picture of Medina Esplanade. The esplanade contained the Hove Baths and Laundry, opened in September 1895. This postcard shows the view looking eastward and the low-roofed swimming pool with the large slogan—'SWIMMING TAUGHT'.

78 The width of the Promenade is clearly illustrated in this postcard which shows the Medina Esplanade looking westwards. In the late 1890s, when this photograph was taken, the publishers of the postcard clearly thought that tampering with the original photograph had some advantage; the shadows of all the objects in the foreground have been removed with the exception of the man on the right and a mystery shadow behind him.

THE LAWNS, HOVE.

79 As late as the early 1920s the pleasures of walking on the lawns and the esplanade are evident. The mid-morning sun has encouraged the promenaders to wear either a hat or bring a sunshade. Even the children must conform, it seems, to this social requirement.

80 This aerial picture of the beach, promenade and lawns of Hove shows how the midday sun brings the people onto the beach for pleasure and health. The bathing machines are still evident, even though this picture was probably taken from an aircraft in the 1920s. The effect of the up-Channel drift and the purpose of the groynes are evident.

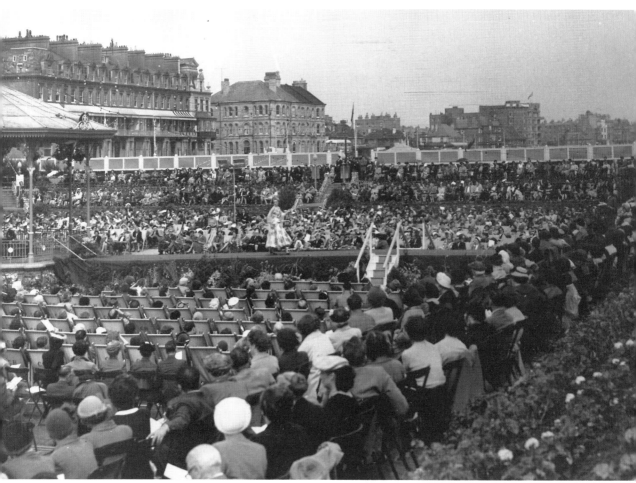

81 In an attempt to keep up with changing tastes in entertainment, the bandstand has been converted, by the addition of a cat-walk, into an open-air fashion show. It is clearly a popular event, as every seat is taken and even the weather smiles on the occasion with sun and a gentle southerly breeze. The costumes are typical of the mid-1950s.

82 The harbour of Shoreham extends into the parish of Aldrington, but the shallow waters of the eastern end were not commercially useful and were developed in the 1930s as a leisure pool for boating. The Lagoon quickly became popular for model sailing boats—often competitively. This picture, taken before 1938, shows model yachts sailing on the Lagoon. Probably because of the speed these yachts could sail at, the photographer has had to touch-up heavily the image of each yacht.

83 This view of the Lagoon looking westward to Aldrington Basin and Shoreham harbour shows the curious mix between leisure activity and the needs of industry. In the foreground couples blithely play pitch-and-put golf while in the background smoke and cranes attest to a different rhythm. In the centre of the picture a three-masted schooner discharges at Aldrington Basin.

84 During the Second World War the whole Sussex coast was considered by the military to be in danger of armed landings or full scale invasion. Accordingly sea defences were arranged. These at Hove, in front of the Lawns, consist of beach defences, anti-tank blocks and two anti-aircraft guns. A half-sunken corrugated bomb shelter has been provided for the defenders. Note the essential enamel mug of 'char' (tea) on the back of the vehicle in the foreground.

85 The anti-tank defences consisted of closely set concrete blocks. Lower down, on the beach anti-infantry obstacles made from building scaffolding were employed. The anti-tank blocks have been capped with paving flags taken from the promenade—presumably to confuse air reconnaissance into thinking they were beach huts. After the war the blocks and barbed wire were used to fill the cuttings on the closed Dyke Railway.

86 The early settlement of Hove was close to the beach and unprotected by elaborate sea walls. This has all changed with the exception of a small group of houses, although of recent date, which still cling to the shoreline. They are known as 'Hove Bungalows', although this is not an obvious description for them as they are multi-storeyed houses. The first of the 'bungalows' was built in 1909.

Public Transport

87 Hove roads were generally laid out with generous width, but there were a number of constrictions and the most notable was 'The Bunion' pictured here. This nickname referred to the out-building of the Brighton Brewery which can be seen just in front of the wagon coming out of George Street onto Church Road. The growing development of Aldrington along New Church Road had added to the volume of horse-drawn traffic and there had been jams and accidents here, but it was the proposal, much disputed, to provide a tramway service that brought the matter to a head. The landowner was not unaware of the strategic importance of this small piece of land and there was much indignation from certain councillors at having to pay some £5,000 for the land. The matter was hotly debated in the council chamber and the letter columns of the local press. Demolition began on 30 May 1902 and was commented on in the *Echo*: 'As a building, the Bunion is quite historical in its way, for it has given rise to as much dispute and unpleasantness as a building well could ... I have seen grave men forsake their gravity, and descend to common forcible household language when discussing the obstruction, and I have watched the light-hearted grow thoughtful and intense as they ran into the wall at dark, or walked upon the narrow pavement in the mud-spray of wayfaring 'buses'.

88 Bennison's livery stables in Brunswick Mews, photographed *c.*1880, combined the provision of transport with accommodation for visiting coachmen and a bar for their entertainment. The sign above the entrance advertises the availability of 'Flys and Broughams'. A fly was a light, covered, public carriage drawn by one horse, also called a hansom or hackney coach. A brougham was a more substantial vehicle for four people.

89 Church Road, and Western Road were by far the busiest roads in turn-of-the-century Hove. There were, despite what we would see as light traffic and slow speed, many accidents to pedestrians, which were fully reported with great concern in the local press. Bolting horses were also a hazard to riders and pedestrians. This picture taken outside the *Albion* at nearly 1.30 p.m. shows two horse buses—one bound for Shoreham, the other for Castle Square in Brighton.

90 (*below*) The view westwards along Church Road still shows what contemporaries thought was heavy traffic. This picture, taken just after 12.10 p.m. (as the Town Hall tells us), shows a mixture of horse and motor buses. The first motor bus services started in 1905, and caused alarm at their speed and the dust thrown up, as well as the vibrations caused by the unmade road surfaces.

91 (*opposite above*) The horse-drawn buses continued after the tramway and trolleybus service had closed. This bus to Castle Square, Brighton, photographed in 1901, is driven by Fred Maslin. The conductor, with his ticket machine slung from his shoulder, is Charles Miller. The thick coat of Mr. Miller, the covered legs and midriff of Mr. Maslin and the bare tree in the background tell us it is wintertime.

92 (*opposite below*) These two Brighton and Hove buses, registration numbers CD103 (on the left) and CD236, were photographed in 1904, probably outside the *Connaught Hotel* in Hove Street. The crew of CD103 was Arthur Dunn (driver) and Charlie Cobden (conductor). The crew of CD236 was Fred Maslin (driver) and George Touque (conductor). Fred Maslin obviously converted happily from driving a horse bus.

93 This group portrait of the Brighton and Hove bus drivers was taken in 1912 at the Conway Street bus station, near Hove railway station. The first petrol fuelled buses started in 1903, but had rapidly expanded to employ at least the 34 drivers in this picture. Two years after this photograph was taken the buses were commandeered for war duty.

94 The tramway between Shoreham and Hove had been controversial from the beginning and had been resisted by the town council who were reluctant to see too much through-traffic. The tram company naturally wanted to link up to its lines in Portslade. The energy efficiency of rail over road haulage is starkly illustrated by this heavy wagon pulled by just two horses. Contrast this with American stage coaches which were much lighter but used six horses to pull it. The last of the Hove to Shoreham horse-drawn trams ran on 6 June 1913.

95 In their effort to provide an acceptable form of public transport, Hove Corporation agreed to an experimental installation of an overhead powered electric trolley bus. The route ran from Hove Station, down Goldstone Villas and George Street to near the Town Hall. The vehicle was not open to the public but ran for Hove and Brighton councillors to assess the system. The bus did not meet with approval, perhaps because it emitted a loud hissing noise when stopped.

96 Goldstone Villas was one of the streets the experimental Cedes electric trolley bus used. The company that supplied the vehicle, Clough Smith and Co., must have been fairly confident in the acceptability of their buses because the overhead lines in the picture appear to have been designed as permanent fixtures.

97 The railway line between Brighton and Shoreham was the first public railway line built in Sussex. It was opened on 12 May 1840. The original station was at Holland Road and was later called Holland Road Halt. The station in this photograph was originally opened as Cliftonville on 1 October 1865. It changed name again to West Brighton when the loop line to Preston Park was opened in 1879. It became Hove Station in 1894 when the Hove Commissioners were superseded by the newly-elected Urban District Council.

98 Hove railway station looks more elegant in this 1890s postcard than it does today. The line between Brighton and Shoreham was built before the London to Brighton line. Electrification, under Southern Railway, was completed on 31 December 1938.

99 With the growth of rail and road traffic the original railway bridge over the upper part of Sackville Road became inadequate. This picture shows the new steel bridge just set in place and the old bridge still partly there. The police officers are preventing the public from using the road as the brickwork is unsafe. The new bridge was constructed by Horseley of Tipton, Staffordshire.

Sport and Entertainment

100 This drawing from the 1820s of Long Barn House, the converted barn on Farmer Rigden's land at the junction of Wilbury and Eaton Roads, shows an informal cricket match in progress. The bowler is the famous William Lillywhite—the Nonpareil, or peerless one. By his new round-arm bowling he revolutionised cricket, taking his wickets at a career average of seven runs. In all five Lillywhites played for Sussex.

101 The sporting interests of Victorian Hove naturally included the manly sports of rowing and sailing. This picture of the annual Hove Regatta taken in 1893 shows the crowd at the water's edge. This was before the new sea wall was built and before the bathing machines had become mixed.

102 The crew of the Foretop No. Two Company and the Elephant Crew pose for a group portrait outside The Battery before a race over the Vallance Course (named after the Vallances of Hove Manor). The Elephant Crew, averaging several stones more than their opponents, won the race in a record time of nine minutes, fifty seconds. The Elephant Crew were: Bennett (stroke), Austin, Vallance, Steel, Denyer and Hollamby. The Foretop Crew comprised: Leppard, W.A. Denyer, Hopwood, Limber, Randall and Poole.

103 Earlier baths had existed at Livingstone Road, but these were essentially for washing rather than swimming. The baths in Medina Esplanade were opened in 1895. Sea bathing was still considered of medical value, so the pool was filled with salt water. The Dutch-gabled building can be seen in the picture of Medina Esplanade (nos.77 and 78).

104 The ornate tile-work of the baths shows clearly in this picture of the interior. The two young women and the young man are being given diving instruction. Besides swimming for pleasure and health, the pool was used for sports, including water-polo. In July 1897 a Hove side lost to Oxford University.

105 (*right*) Open-air activities were popular pastimes for the Victorians and Edwardians and open-air concerts were one of the most popular. The band this evening was the Fourth Royal Irish Dragoon Guards. Entrance was 1d. which gave you the use of a chair 'if available'. The band was scheduled to play on the Brunswick Lawns and the Western Lawns. Even then bicycles were chained.

106 (*below*) The Irish Guards in the previous picture also played at the Western Lawns (west of the King Alfred). In this slightly later picture the audience is assembling for an afternoon concert. Whether by coincidence or because there was a rally, the cars parked in the Kingsway are 'bull-nosed Morrises'. This model was one of Britain's most successful cars in the 1920s. This picture was probably taken in 1925 when the car was at its height of popularity.

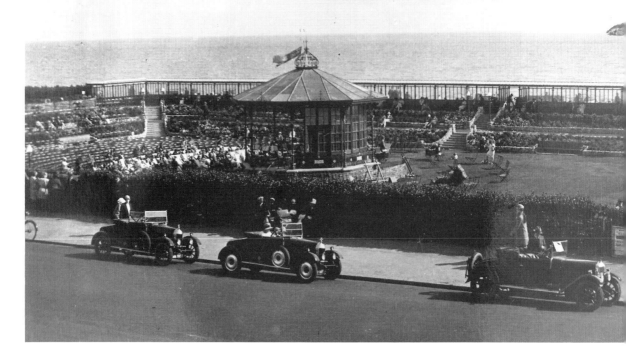

107 (*below*) Later still, in the 1940s, the bandstand was still in use for entertainment—in this case *al fresco* dancing! Originally the bandstand was open on all sides but the prevailing westerly winds proved too much for the bands and the windward side was glazed. The chairs have been replaced with deck-chairs.

108 Hove people seem to have been very keen, perhaps keener than most, on sport. This may account for the town hosting the only League Football club, the County Cricket Club and Sussex's only greyhound stadium. Football was a popular sport from the 1880s onward and amateur teams flourished, especially in the 1920s when this photograph of the Old Hoverians Football Club was taken.

LBION V NORTHAMPTON - 1921

WILES

6

109 The county's only league club has played at the Goldstone Ground since 1902. The local photographer, T. Wiles, would take photographs of the crowd before the game started and try to have prints ready by the whistle to take orders for copies. This picture was taken at the game against Northampton in 1921.

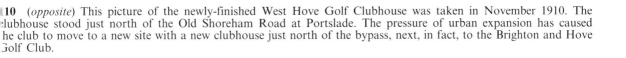

10 (*opposite*) This picture of the newly-finished West Hove Golf Clubhouse was taken in November 1910. The clubhouse stood just north of the Old Shoreham Road at Portslade. The pressure of urban expansion has caused the club to move to a new site with a new clubhouse just north of the bypass, next, in fact, to the Brighton and Hove Golf Club.

11 (*opposite below*) The opening of the new golf club was marked with an exhibition match between two of the club's top players, D.F.S. Smith and the Rev. Sulllivan, and two professional golfers, Bland and Waldon.

12 (*below*) The match attracted a large crowd. Here Waldon is putting. The practice of referring to professionals by their surnames only was a form of snobbery to distinguish them from gentlemen, and women, who played for fun rather than money.

113 The earliest popula
form of flying was by hot a
balloon. As now they were
popular recreational thril
This balloon, in the ground
of Brooker Hall (then th
home of the widow of Joh
Oliver Vallance and now th
museum and art gallery), wa
photo-graphed in summer c
1905.

114 The slow speed of the earlier aircraft meant that a race between them was a practical spectator event. On 13 May 1911 such a race took place at Brighton and Hove and according to the local paper 'brought wonderment and delight' and 'gave an amazing demonstration of man's conquest of the air'. The leading aircraft are seen here approaching Aldrington.

15 This aerial view of Hove Park was taken 57 years after its opening in 1906. The provision of 12 tennis courts and a bowling green illustrate the reasons for the resentment the provision of the park caused amongst the working-class residents of Hove, who argued that the facilities were intended primarily for the better off and better leisured residents.

16 The Ice Rink, by Hove Station, opened in 1929. The rink stayed open for only three years before the craze for skating gave way to the next new thing in entertainment—the talkies. It was converted into a cinema and, after the boom years of the talkies, it was converted once again to meet yet another craze—ten-pin bowling. It has since been demolished.

117 (*left*) Many neighbourhood public houses used to arrange an annual outing like the one pictured here. The men (exclusively men) are dressed up, with buttonholes and white shirts. A football is being taken for a game later on—there are more than enough for two full sides—and in the back row the group's accordion player proudly presents his instrument.

118 (*below left*) Socially the most important Hove activity was promenading. It was for this that the extensive Lawns had been laid out, which attracted the more genteel visitors to the town. In late Victorian and Edwardian times it was the 'done' thing to attend the outdoor church service on Brunswick Lawns and then mix socially on the Lawns. This picture was taken shortly after the First World War near the Peace Statue which stands at the border between Hove and Brighton.

119 (*below*) The midday sun has brought out the town's fashionable people for a promenade on the Lawns. The little boy with the dog is wearing the then fashionable sailor suit. The older women carry parasols, while the younger women in the forefront are more daring!

Cinema History

120 The Empire, in Haddington Street, was Hove's first cinema. The building was converted from a rifle range and a general hall. It served as a cinema for more than 20 years before closing down in 1933. The site is now occupied by a supermarket. The Empire sat 300 people in the stalls and a balcony.

121 The first manager of the Empire was Robert Flint, seen in this picture seated in his motor car. This open-topped vehicle doubled as a mobile camera platform and was used to shoot local scenes which were then shown at the Empire. In 1912 seat prices were: pit 3d. and balcony 6d.

122 Eddie Scrivens was one of the earliest movie fans. Fired with enthusiasm by seeing an early film on the West Pier, he persuaded his father to open the Empire. The first performance was on 10 December 1910. Eddie, shown here in the foyer, was the projectionist and also the cameraman for the films shot locally. He later became manager and stayed with the Empire until its closure.

123 The Kine Studio, photographed in 1911, was George Albert Smith's second purpose-built film studio. His first studio at St Ann's Well, which he leased before it became a park, was the world's first film studio. Prior to this filming had been done outdoors. His other great claim to fame is as the inventor of the first practical colour cine film—'Kinemacolor'.

The Devil's Dyke and the Dyke Railways

124   The Devil's Dyke, although just outside the northern boundary of Hove, has had a significant influence on the town. The Dyke is supposed by legend to have been dug by the Devil in order to flood the Weald with sea water and silence the bells of the numerous churches. To succeed he had to complete the task by dawn but was tricked by a hastily-lit light into abandoning the task.

125   The popularity of Devil's Dyke with Victorian tourists, ever keen on excursions, led inevitably to the commercial exploitation of the site. The first inn on the summit was built in 1817, but it was William Thacker who first brought effective entrepreneurial skills to the task. This print shows his first establishment, built soon after 1835.

View from the Devil's Dyke looking West.

126 This engraving from the 1830s shows the popularity of the Dyke among the leisured classes. Picnicking is in progress and one member of the party is using a telescope to scan the North Downs and beyond. Westward along the ridge of the downs is the tree-capped Chanctonbury Hill. The artist has dramatised the hills by exaggerating their form.

127 This print shows the *Dyke Hotel* about 1876. William Thacker took over the early inn on the site in 1835 and remained as proprietor for 50 years. He built the hotel shown in this print 1871. The fashionable horse-drawn wagonette in the front of the hotel was known as a 'char a banc', French for 'a wagon with benches'.

128 This winter view of the hotel shows that Thacker's original building has been extended. Over the years fresh attractions were added to the natural wonders of the Devil's Dyke and the wonderful views. These included bandstands, an observatory and a camera obscura. Swingboats can be seen to the left of the photograph.

129 Amongst the attractions at the hotel in the late 1890s was this merry-go-round or set of gallopers. They were usually steam-driven with a steam-powered organ worked by giant punched cards. These cards were like mechanical computer programmes, with the punched holes acting as digital instructions to the organ to play a particular note. These fairground attractions are associated with William Thacker's successor, Mr. Hubbard.

130 The success of the *Dyke Hotel* easily led to the idea of building a railway from the existing railway network to the Dyke. Given the gradient, this was an engineering challenge. But the railway was built and the first train ran in September 1887. This picture shows a train arriving at the Dyke Station, which was still some sixty metres (200 ft.) below the summit.

131 (*above*) Trains for Dyke Station started from Brighton but the true beginning of the Dyke Railway was at Aldrington, where points just beyond the platform end diverted the trains northwards onto the new line. The would-be passenger is Ms. Judy Dale (Osborne), former local history librarian and co-author of the first walker's guide to the disused line. The last train ran in 1938 so Judy is over forty years too late!

132 (*right*) To add to the natural attractions of the Dyke and help complete the journey to the summit from Dyke Station, the proprietor of the *Dyke Hotel*, Mr. Hubbard, built this cableway. It opened in 1894 and was immediately popular, although it made little sense in transport terms. The return fare was 6d. The cable-car is half-way across.

133 (*above*) This close-up of the northern tower shows how the cable was suspended. The cable car, powered by a diesel oil engine, passed through the pylons which were just under two hundred metres apart. The full length of the cable was 366 metres. The cableway captured the imagination of many and was immensely popular, although there were some environmental objections.

134 To add a further attraction and to tap a new market in the Wealden villages, in 189 Mr. Hubbard built a funicular railway from the Dyke to Poynings village. The two cars were connected by a cable and, with their counterweight supported by an engine, travelled at three m.p.h. Now two short walks and three railways joined the villages to Brighton.

135 This picture, showing a horse-drawn bus from Brighton entering the grounds of the newly commercially developed *Dyke Hotel* site, shows most incredibly, a fourth Dyke railway! This is the fairground Switchback Railway seen in the middleground of the picture.

The Canal and Aldrington Basin

136 The import of timber for house-building and furniture-making was an important trade because of the population growth of local towns as well as the newly-growing cities. This postcard shows a smart three-masted schooner at the timber docks and a ferryman sculling across the Canal to pick up his fares.

137 The Basin or Canal became a part of Hove when Aldrington parish was added to Hove. This picture shows the two principal import trades: the sailing ship the *Alice Goodhue* of Newcastle has unloaded Baltic timber and the steam collier *Trent* of Hull is unloading coal into horse-drawn tip carts. The row-boat is on a sight-seeing trip.

Some Schools

138 The passing of the Education Act of 1870 saw the beginning of provision for education for those whose parents were unable to afford adequate private education. In Hove this led to the building of schools in the comparatively less affluent areas. Connaught Road School opened in 1884 and this picture shows the female pupils and staff in the late 1880s.

39 The younger school children were educated together, and not separated by gender like those in the previous picture. This group picture of the younger children and staff was taken in 1885. Dress and hair styles are more flamboyant than in the previous picture, with two boys dressed in the then popular sailor suits.

140 This group portrait of the staff and children of Aldrington Church of England School in Portland Road, taken in 1909, shows the children slightly less formally dressed than in the earlier picture of Connaught School. The teacher is Miss Johnson.

Events

141   This picture of the 1912 Agricultural Show reminds us that much of what has become Hove was once farmland. In fact as the town grew it became more of a centre for outlying farmlands than when it was a small village. Before the First World War regular agricultural and mechanical exhibitions filled the Town Hall.

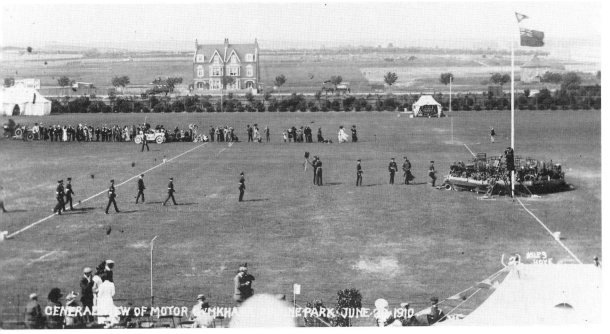

GENERAL VIEW OF MOTOR GYMKHANA THE PARK JUNE 2 1910

142 As motor transport began to replace horse transport the traditional gymkhana (horsemanship displays) was adopted by sporting motorists. This event in Marine Park, Aldrington in June 1910 is enjoying fine weather but with a stiff breeze. The band (no Hove outdoor event was complete without one) is returning. The bus to Shoreham has just passed the house in the middle distance.

143 One Sunday morning, after the fashionable church parade, life on the Lawns was enlivened by the arrival of this Bristol biplane. On Sunday 21 May 1911 the pilot, Mr. Graham Gilmour, with a passenger, Mr. Gordon England, landed on Brunswick Lawns. The picture was taken by a young woman, Miss E. Lennock, who recalled that the plane crashed some two years later.

144 This triumphal arch was erected in Western Road at the eastern entrance to Hove in 1888 to mark the visit of the Prince of Wales. The inscription on the arch reads: 'To the town of Hove a "hundred thousand welcomes" '. The lettering on the left is a translation of Hove's motto, *Floreat Hova*, 'Hove shall flourish'. His popularity with the people remained when he became Edward VII on the death of his mother, Queen Victoria.

145 Edward VII died on 6 May 1910. He lay in state from the 11th until the 20th when he was buried at St George's Chapel, Windsor. This crowd scene shows the grief on the faces of the people as they attend a memorial service on what would otherwise have been a cheerful late Spring day.

146 Like most of the south-coast towns, Hove suffered from sporadic bomber and fighter attacks in the Second World War. This picture shows the damaged sustained to houses in Nizell's Avenue and the rescue workers looking for survivors.

Commercial Life

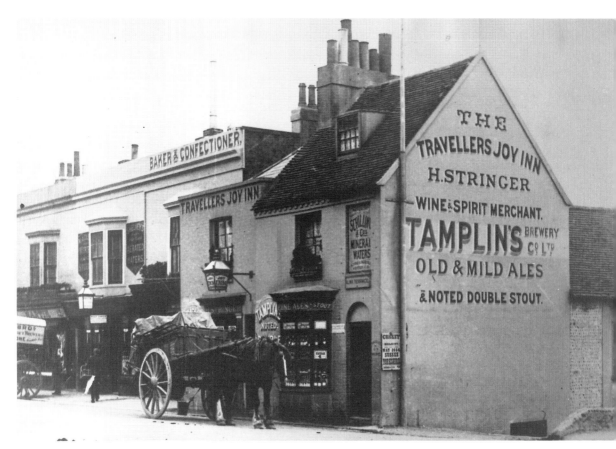

147 The *Travellers Joy* was one of the earlier pubs in the newly-developed Hove. This photograph, taken in 1894, shows the small terrace, Alma Terrace, of commercial properties that stood next to the larger north-facing terraces in what was to become Kingsway. The gable end of the inn displays a poster advertising a cricket match against Yorkshire which Sussex, sadly, lost.

148 There were several brewerie in Hove and brewing was profitable business, then as now This picture shows Tamplin Brewery in Osborne Street lookin towards Church Road and Scott pianoforte shop, which had pianc for sale or for hire. The Vallanc family in nearby Hove Mano were major brewers in this area Tamplins were later taken over b Watneys and then re-forme locally as the Phoenix Brewery.

49 This turn-of-century photograph of Church Road was taken from the junction of Sackville Road, Hove Street nd New Church Road. It shows clearly the commercial activity that the building of Cliftonville and Aldrington had enerated. The horse-drawn Portslade bus has just passed the Brighton Castle Square bus. The handcarts, buses and icycles begin to give a hint of the traffic that was to come.

150 Apart from the lack of traffic and the replacement of the Town Hall, this scene in Church Road has changed little from the time this picture was taken. Forfars bread shop is still there today and the *Albion Inn*, too. The landlord, A. Grinver, proudly proclaims himself.

151 The store in Western Road opened by William Hill in the late 1870s was one of the symbols, together with Palmeira House, which served to distinguish Hove from Brighton. The elegance and comprehensiveness of these stores were seen as sufficient reason to shop in Hove rather than Brighton. This picture, from *c.*1906, shows the store divided into separate shops. It would soon adopt the departmental layout.

152   Blatchington Road was planned as the shopping area for the Stanford Estate and, to a lesser extent, the northern part of Cliftonville. Although the Stanford Estate could boast grand roads like Goldstone and Denmark Villas, much of the estate consisted of housing for the working population. To meet their needs second-hand furniture suppliers, like F. Wright, set up in business. This picture shows their early delivery wagon.

153   The Stanford Estate started developing in the 1870s and continued to grow up until the 1890s. F. Wright began his business in 1875 at the beginning of the building boom. As well as offering a removal service (an obvious requirement on a growing estate) his firm were cabinet makers and suppliers of beds, baths and prams, as well as other requirements for new tenants. This canvas-covered lorry, photographed *c*.1914, with its fold-back driver's canopy and solid-rubber tyres, shows the firm's growing prosperity.

154 As the firm grew and his family grew, the sons were incorporated into the business, and so the firm became F. Wright and Sons. The firm also acquired additional premises in Arthur Street near Aldrington Halt Station, which was available as a depository, or furniture store. The firm's new lorry is a Daimler.

155 Blatchington Road and George Street form one of several shopping centres in Hove. Blatchington Road was once called North Place, because it marked the northern limit of buildings in the old village of Hove. Work on the new street began in 1870. The photograph, which was taken in 1959, shows the junction between Blatchington Road and George Street and Goldstone Villas. The street lighting is suspended above the road and the pedestrian crossing is of the pre-zebra type. This crossing was called a Belisha Beacon crossing after the government minister, Hore Belisha, who introduced the striped beacon with an orange globe light on top.

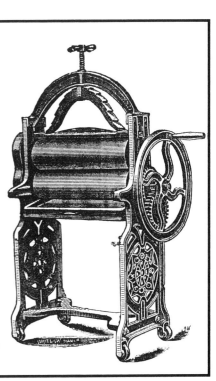
56 The mangle was a typical Victorian piece of machinery. Engineered in heavy cast iron and built to last a thousand years, it was as desirable a household gadget then as the automatic washing machine is today. Without mangles it would have been difficult to dry clothes in winter. Blackford and Co. were in the business of supplying mangles, prams, bassinettes and other household goods and services to the householders on the Stanford Estate. They offered hire service or a hire-purchase agreement.

157 The eastern end of Church Road at George Street and Blatchington Road was the main shopping place for a large area of Hove so this shop of James Edward was a very well sited. Edward's shop was general clothing shop catering for men and women and including tailoring services. At this stage of his business his premises are used to advertise W.T. Nye's store in George Street.

158 A few years later and James Edward has acquired his own large sign in place of Nye's and has revamped the display lighting. Notice the line of sporting caps in the doorway. In the George Street side of the shop a poster advertising a Sussex cricket match is displayed.

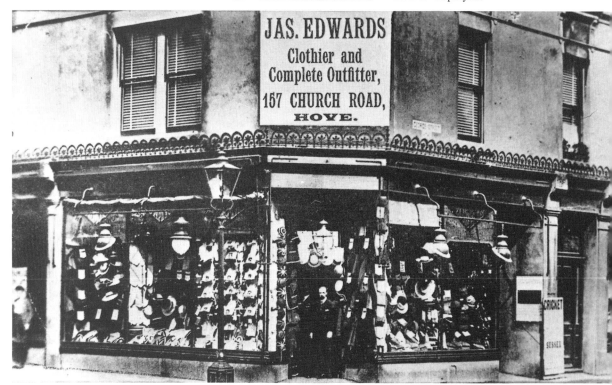

Town Affairs

159 The first Hove Town Hall was originally Brunswick Town Hall and served the Brunswick Commissioners. When the Hove Commissioners took over responsibility for Brunswick it became Hove Town Hall. The growing population, especially the development of Cliftonville, called for a larger and more central building. Land was purchased from the Stanford Estate and the architect Alfred Waterhouse was appointed. Waterhouse was something of a high priest of Victorian Gothic, as his buildings like the Natural History Museum at Kensington and the Pru' (Prudential Insurance Office) in Holborn show, although the Town Hall was a subdued example of his elaborate style. It was built by Chappel of London and completed in 1882. The Town Hall was destroyed by fire in 1966.

160 This print shows the Town Hall from the east and shows the Tisbury Road face. The building occupied the whole frontage between Tisbury Road and Norton Road. The Norton Road extension was large and contained a parade ground for the Hove police. A major feature of the Town Hall was the clock tower with its four faces with 2.3 metre dials and a set of bells with a repertoire of 14 patriotic songs.

161 This group portrait of the Hove police was taken in October 1884 outside the Norton Wing of the newly-built Town Hall. Standing on the left, in a pill-box hat and frock coat, is Detective Inspector Berry. He was to leave the Hove police in March 1887 for the post of Head Constable of the Guildford Borough Police. The men are wearing their winter uniforms with strong leather belts from which they hung their 'bull's-eye' lanterns when on night duty.

162 This fine portrait, probably taken *c.*1870, is of Jesse Burchell, the first Sergeant of Police in the Hove Police Force. He is wearing a frock coat uniform with the modern-style helmet that succeeded the earlier top hat. There is a record of a Constable Burchell of the Brunswick police force assisting in the ceremony of 'beating the bounds' in 1839.

163 Captain Terry, His Majesty's Chief Inspector of Mounted Police (on foot), inspecting the Hove police in June 1911. The contract for supplying and stabling the police horses at this period was held by Messrs. Thomas Tilling Limited. The stables were at the bottom of Holland Road on the site now occupied by an extension to the *Brunswick Hotel.* Tillings held the contract from 1909 until shortly before the outbreak of the First World War.

164 The first fire station in Hove was a shed in Brunswick Street West but, by the time this photograph was taken *c*.1905, the Hove Fire Brigade station was in George Street. The firemen are demonstrating a newly-acquired steam pump. At this time the engine was still drawn by horses.

165 As a training and public relation exercises the Hove Fire Brigade demonstrated the efficiency of their new pump by hosing down the Town Hall. There is a certain irony in this, because the Town Hall did eventually burn down in 1966.

166 Until 1906, when this picture was taken, the sewerage
system for Brighton and Hove consisted of a series of
north-south sewers, some of which had once discharged
onto the beach, but which had, with the growth of the
towns, been connected to an east-west intercepting sewer
running along the sea front. The addition to the Borough
of Hove of the parish of Aldrington, and more particularly
the spectacular population growth of Aldrington, caused
the borough engineer in 1903 to bring before the council
a proposal for dealing with the present and anticipated
problem. In 1861 the population of the parish was six, by
1901 it had risen to 6,893. The borough surveyor estimated
that it would be 30,000 in 1939. He proposed that a new
sewer be built along the Aldrington sea front to join the
western end of the intercepting sewer at the bottom of
Hove Street.

167 Hove borough surveyor's proposal to build an
extension to the intercepting sewer caused considerable
concern in Brighton because the large additional load of
sewerage from Aldrington, especially if the surveyor's
population estimates were correct, threatened to overload
the system. Worse, because of the levels of the sewers, the
overload would discharge mostly at Brighton. The Brighton
Intercepting and Outfall Sewers Board received technical
advice that the system would not cope and recommended
a separate discharge at Aldrington or Shoreham. Hove
borough maintained that the board had a duty to receive
the sewerage from Aldrington as it was now part of Hove.
This was disputed and the case was appealed all the way
to the House of Lords who found in Hove's favour. The
picture, taken in 1906, shows the new intercepting sewer
striking one of the old sewers which it was designed to
link with. The concrete lump from the old sewer weighed
two tons.

168 The Brighton Dispensary was financed from charitable sources. Dispensaries were provided to give hospital treatment to the poor. The Hove branch was opened because the growth in population justified a hospital in Hove. A branch of the dispensary was opened at Farm Road in Brunswick. As Hove developed westward, the need for a new hospital became pressing and the controlling committee built a new hospital at Sackville Road in 1888. This picture shows the impressive gabled front of the new hospital.

169 The new hospital began on a sound financial basis, but perhaps because there was less glamour in providing funds to maintain, rather than to build, a hospital, it was not long before it was in financial difficulties. This picture, taken *c*.1910, just before 'elevenses' (as the clock shows us), illustrates the neat and airy layout of the purpose-built hospital. The hospital still serves today as Hove General Hospital.

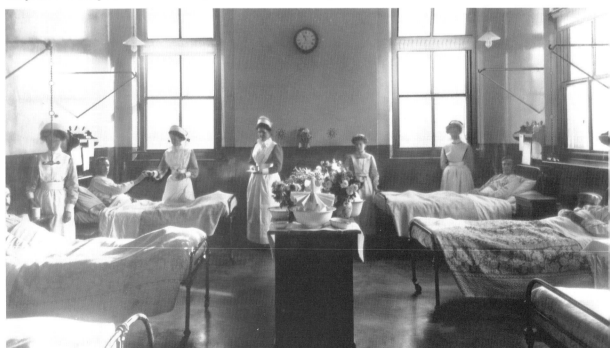

170 During the First World War the hospital was naturally used for nursing the vast numbers of casualties that the grim battles of northern France produced. So great was the pressure to accommodate the wounded that an annexe to the hospital was created in nearby Portland Road—known colloquially as 'The Hut'.

171   The success of Brighton and Hove as pleasant places to visit had from the early 18th century been partly based on the availability of subscription libraries. With the growth in literacy among the working population and the growth of the public library movement, pressure was put upon local authorities to provide a free library. The first public library was in Grand Avenue, but the need for larger premises quickly became apparent and the library moved to Third Avenue. The Scottish-born American steel baron, Andrew Carnegie, spent some of his vast wealth on building libraries and the present library in Church Road was opened on 8 July 1908, built with money given by him.

172   The new public library was opened in 1908. Earlier libraries had been designed to keep the public away from the shelves as there was some concern about letting the common people have free access to ideas that might threaten the establishment. Hove library was designed to allow free access to the books but provide the maximum staff supervision of the borrowers. This indicated a semi-circular lending library with the staff located mid-circle for easy supervision. This plan can be seen in this picture of the Wolseley Room, which was a first-floor addition to the original design. The room was paid for by Frances Wolseley, daughter of Lord Wolseley, Commander in Chief of the Army (W.S. Gilbert's 'model of a modern major-general') to house her father's papers and her own local studies archive.

173 The decision to spend public money on a park for Hove proved a very contentious matter. First there was the question of need, second the question of location, and thirdly the question of cost. Various locations were suggested and all found strong opponents on the borough council. These debates, unusually, found the proposers of a park supported by the councillors representing the moneyed interest (not previously noted for proposing expenditure), while opposition to a park came from the representatives of the working people. This seeming contradiction is explained by the eventual location of Hove Park—which favoured the more plush area of Hove. This picture was taken in 1906 just prior to the formal opening.

174 The tree-planting plan for Hove Park consisted almost entirely of native trees—elm, plane, oak, beech, she-oak, chestnuts, sycamore and holly among them. In all, over seven thousand trees and shrubs were planted. This photograph, again taken just before the opening in spring 1906 and looking towards the north-east corner and Tredcroft Road, shows part of the extensive planting.

175 After all the landscaping and planting the opening of Hove Park just had to be a grand event. Accompanied by mounted police and with a nautical guard of honour, the procession of carriages is just arriving at the park. The formal opening was carried out on 24 May 1906 by the Mayor, Alderman Bruce Morison.

176 This is St Ann's Well, the site of the chalybeate spring. The spring water contained salts of irons which were considered to be good for health. Dr. Russell, who had made sea bathing so popular, advised some of his patients to use the spring and its popularity led eventually to the building of this proper pump house in 1891, complete with Ionic portico. There is a legend about the name of the well. Lady Annefrida was betrothed to Wolmuth of Hollingbury. While he was away at war Black Harold of Patcham sought to marry her, and on Wolnuth's return from the wars, slew him just west of Brightelmstone. Lady Annefrida visited the grave of Wolmuth every day and her copious tears caused the well named after her. She died three years later and was buried on the same spot as Wolnuth. The sinking of artesian wells nearby has caused the well to dry up. The pump house decayed and was pulled down in 1935.

177 The Furze Hill entrance to St Ann's Well Gardens led to the 'Wild Garden', an area of informal parkland without formal flower beds and lawns. The entrance fee was 3d. This entrance building replaced an earlier one with a conical roof that 'used to glory in its mossy exterior' (Porter's *History of Hove*, 1897). Under the eaves of the gate house there appear to be vending machines.

178 This old ship's figurehead was place in St Ann's Well Gardens to commemora the new king's accession to the throne in 191 King George V had followed a naval care until the death of his older brother requir him to take up state duties and he w popularly known as the Sailor King.

179 The King Alfred was built in 1939 a Hove Marina but was immediate requisitioned by the RNVR an commissioned as HMS *King Alfred*. Durin the war years 22,500 officers from all ov the empire were trained at King Alfred. Th building was re-opened in August 1946 b Admiral Layton as a sports centre.

80 More than in most towns, Hove's cemetery is a highly visible feature because one of the two east-west routes through the town bisects it. The first part, south of the Old Shoreham Road, was opened in 1882. The first burial was that of Frederick Tooth on 15 January 1882. Altogether the cemetery covers 45 acres. This picture shows the chapel, which is still used for committal services.

81 One corner of the cemetery in Old Shoreham Road is reserved for Jewish burials. The Jewish community have played an important part in the life of Hove and particularly in the development of the town. The area around Palmeira Square was developed by Baron de Goldsmid e de Palmeira. He was the first Jewish baronet.

182 Hove cemetery contains the remains of many distinguish[ed] and famous people. This is the grave of Martin Leonard Landfr[ied] who, at 15 years old, sounded The Charge—the Charge of [the] Light Brigade at Balaclava, when, in Tennyson's words 'into [the] Valley of Death rode the six hundred'. Landfried had [a] distinguished career, serving in the Indian mutiny and retiring [as] Trumpet Major.

183 The great English batsman, Sir Jack Hobbs, is buried in Hove, together with his wife and daughter . His playing career for Cambridgeshire, Surrey and England spanned the first quarter of this century. Sir Jack opened the Tate Memorial gates at the County Cricket Ground in 1958 in commemoration of the Sussex cricketer, Maurice Tate.

Index

Roman numerals refer to pages in the introduction and arabic numerals to individual illustrations.